PLAN COLOMBIA: THE STRATEGIC AND OPERATIONAL IMPERATIVES

Gabriel Marcella

April 2001

FOREWORD

The crisis in Colombia is the most compelling challenge the United States faces in the Western Hemisphere. The United States is committed to helping Colombia fight its struggle against the violence and corruption engendered by the traffic in narcotics. This report examines the strategic theory within *Plan Colombia*, the master plan which the government of Colombia developed to strengthen democracy through peace, security, and economic development. In this timely paper, Dr. Gabriel Marcella argues that the United States and the international community must support this beleaguered nation. He cautions, however, that the main responsibility for success lies with the Colombians. They must mobilize the national resources and make the sacrifices to win back the country from the narco-traffickers, the insurgents, and the paramilitaries. To that end, *Plan Colombia* is a well-conceived strategy that must be sustained for the long term.

This is the first of a series of monographs stemming from a major conference held in Miami, Florida, on February 1-2, 2001. That conference, entitled "Implementing Plan Colombia: Strategic and Operational Imperatives," was cosponsored by The Dante B. Fascell North-South Center at the University of Miami and the Strategic Studies Institute at the U.S. Army War College. The intent was to clarify issues, focus the debate, and learn from it. We are pleased to publish this monograph in the hope that it may contribute to a resolution of Colombia's problems through greater dialogue and debate.

DOUGLAS C. LOVELACE, JR.
Director
Strategic Studies Institute

FOREWORD

This monograph by Dr. Gabriel Marcella is eloquent testimony to the immense stake which the United States has in the outcome of Colombia's multifaceted crisis. The prolongation of Colombia's troubles and their potential deepening present a threat to the stability of an entire region. The problem goes well beyond the question of illegal drug production and supply. It means the possible reversal of major, positive developments in Central and South America through the 1990s which include democratization, growth through freer markets, and economic integration through free trade agreements leading to an eventual Free Trade Area of the Americas. Both the Clinton administration and, now, the Bush administration have shown a commitment to help Colombia because it is in our own national interest to do so. It is incumbent upon the people of Colombia principally, but also the international community, to stay the course during a multi-year effort of grand proportions.

That part is not easy for Washington, given over, as this country often is, to short-term thinking. *Plan Colombia* recognizes realistically the need for patience and determination in pursuit of a broad range of initiatives for years to come. Leadership will be required to get that point across to electorates and legislators who demand quicker results than may be possible. The United States, through the commitment of $1.3 billion, has become engaged in the program. But this moment is, as Winston Churchill said at a certain turning point in World War II, "not the end or even the beginning of the end, but possibly the end of the beginning."

The Dante B. Fascell North-South Center is pleased to collaborate with the U.S. Army War College. We offer, through a recent conference and now through a series of studies such as this, an ongoing analysis of the policy issues which are of critical importance to this country and to the Western Hemisphere.

Ambler Moss
Director
Dante B. Fascell North-South Center
University of Miami

BIOGRAPHICAL SKETCH OF THE AUTHOR

GABRIEL MARCELLA teaches strategy in the Department of National Security and Strategy at the U.S. Army War College. He previously served as International Affairs Advisor to the Commander-in-Chief, United States Southern Command. His recent publications include: *Warriors in Peacetime: The Military and Democracy in Latin America*, "Colombia's Three Wars: U.S. Strategy at the Crossroads," *Security Cooperation in the Western Hemisphere: Resolving the Ecuador-Peru Conflict* (coauthor); "The Presidential Advisory System and the Making of Latin American Policy," and "The Interagency Process and National Security: Forward Into the 21st Century." His current research interests focus on the Colombian crisis, national security decisionmaking, and the strategic dimensions of civil-military relations in times of crisis and war. He is a frequent commentator on Latin American security issues and U.S. policy in the printed and electronic media.

PLAN COLOMBIA: THE STRATEGIC AND OPERATIONAL IMPERATIVES

> Colombia today would be a completely different country if it had not suffered for the last twenty years all the perverse effects of narco-trafficking . . . it would be more secure, more governable, and more democratic.[1]

Colombia's Travails.

Colombia is the most difficult challenge facing the United States in the hemisphere. Washington's prestigious Inter-American Dialogue affirmed in late 2000: "No country in Latin America outside of Mexico will command greater U.S. policy attention than Colombia."[2] It has long been besieged by internal conflict. But the appetite for cocaine and heroin in the United States (where 3.5 million people are addicted to cocaine and up to 12 million use illegal drugs), Europe, Canada, Asia, and Latin America feeds a veritable killing machine that annually takes the lives of over 3,000 (over 40,000 in the last 10 years). Nearly 2,500 kidnappings took place in Colombia in 2000, securing once again that country's first rank in that dreadful business.

Violence has displaced over 1.5 million people caught in the crossfire of shooting, threats, and counter-threats, from the insurgents and paramilitary vigilantes. Its destructiveness intensifies poverty. The insecurity makes normal life practically impossible for Colombians of all classes.[3]

Colombia's problems also raise deep concerns in Ecuador, Peru, Venezuela, Panama, and Brazil about spillover violence, corruption, ecological damage, and criminal activity.[4] There is fear of the "balloon effect," the threat that coca cultivation could move across borders (and back into Peru and Bolivia) should Colombia dramatically reduce cultivation.[5] Moreover, the violence and uncertainty about the future contribute to the steepest economic decline in two generations, with 20 percent unemployment for the year 2000.

Insecurity and contagious pessimism about the future drive thousands of Colombians to seek opportunity and personal and family security abroad, especially in the United States. A leading intellectual expresses the current grim national mood in Colombia:

> . . . no idea, no ideology, no leader, no force, no institution of national scale that might try to convince us, provokes admiration or moves the collective enthusiasm . . . A Congress out of touch with reality . . . An opposition of beggars and actors . . . A criminal insurgency without ideas. A murderous right . . . frightened intellectuals . . . Businessmen on the defensive and a "civil society" which no longer exists.[6]

The institutional capacity of the state to deal with the problems of governance and public security is manifestly weak. Colombia's collective troubles are a powerful combination of the lack of authority, legitimacy, and governance. The leading scholar on the violence, Eduardo Pizarro of the National University of Colombia and research professor at the University of Notre Dame, refers in Spanish to the partial collapse of the state and the ominous emergence of the solution from the right as *derechización*, which implies increasing popular support for the illegal right-wing paramilitaries in a society looking for alternatives. This is a common historical pattern in societies riven by deep conflict. As the political center weakens and public security declines, a society will naturally look for security from the right.[7]

Plan Colombia and the United States.

The United States has been assisting Colombia for decades, but the imperative changed dramatically in 1997-98 as Colombia displaced Peru and Bolivia as the major source of coca production. Because these two

Colombian neighbors succeeded in sharply reducing coca cultivation, the enterprise moved north into southern and eastern Colombia. These remote areas are lightly populated and practically free of such manifestations of the Colombian state as the judicial system, police, military, roads, schools, medical service, markets, and credit facilities. Indeed, over 40 percent of the national territory is outside the control of the central government, thus posing a serious challenge to national unity throughout the history of independent Colombia. In this area outside the government's control, soil, temperature, and moisture conditions can produce four crops of coca in 12 months. Today close to 300,000 acres in various areas throughout Colombia annually produce an estimated 520 metric tons compared with 245 produced by Peru and Bolivia combined. The following table shows the dramatic shift in production patterns. Until 1997 most of the coca was grown in Peru and Bolivia, while coca base was shipped to Colombia for processing and distribution.

	1995	1996	1997	1998	1999
Peru	460	435	325	240	175
Bolivia	240	215	200	150	70
Colombia	230	300	350	435	520
Totals	930	950	875	825	765

Table 1. Andean Potential Cocaine Production (Metric Tons).

The Colombian production areas of Putumayo, Caquetá, Guaviare are, moreover, dominated by insurgents known as the FARC (*Fuerzas Armadas Revolucionarias Colombianas*) and the paramilitary vigilantes. The FARC are 15,000-20,000 strong, of whom some 6,000 may be forcibly recruited children, according to the UNICEF representative in Colombia.[8] The paramilitary groups (*autodefensas)* are some 6,000 in strength and growing. The tenacity with which the FARC fought to preserve its control over the coca production areas in Putumayo department in the fall of 2000 clearly demonstrates that the narcotics-guerrilla nexus is no longer a myth.[9] Estimates run as high as $500 million per year for the amount of money that goes into insurgent coffers from the coca business through extortion and war taxes. This amount, enough to fund a formidable war machine, allowed FARC battallion-sized formations in 1997-98 to inflict serious defeats upon the Colombian army. The paramilitaries also depend upon coca proceeds, with their leader, Carlos Castaño, asserting them to be 70 percent of their war chest. Some analysts argue that the FARC will not be strategically defeated by eliminating the drug money going to the war chest. This is because nearly 50 percent of their income (which does not come from coca) would be unaffected, allowing them to maintain a significant tempo of military operations.[10]

In the United States each year illegal drug use kills some 52,000 persons. The costs of health care, accidents, and lost productivity reach $110 billion. The illegal drug trade generates violence and corrupts wherever it touches, from Mexico, through Central America, Panama, and the Caribbean states, reaching even the highest circles of governments. A senior U.S. diplomat who served in Colombia estimates that two-thirds to three-fourths of the members of the Colombian Congress are corrupt. Thus at stake for the international community are the core principles of democratic community—the rule of law, the inviolability of international borders, and the security of the individual and society. Illegal drugs contribute significantly to the $600 billion global money-laundering economy.

Colombia, three times the size of Montana with a population of 40 million, is important to the United States in far more positive terms. Overall bilateral trade is $10 billion per year, and Colombia will play a key role in the anticipated economic integration of the hemisphere, the visionary Free Trade Area of the Americas, targeted for 2005. Until its recent troubles, the country was considered one of the leading democracies in Latin America. However, under the enormous strain of conflict, its deep flaws as a democracy have become salient: corruption, a totally dysfunctional judicial system (despite having eight times the number of judges the United States has for every 100,000 people), and an ineffective governmental reach across a vast territory.[11]

A decisive turn in U.S. policy began when Andrés Pastrana assumed the presidency in 1998. Having campaigned on a promise to end the three decades of war, he declared dramatically: "For peace I risk everything." He soon embarked on a risky peace process. In January 1999 he granted the FARC a 16,000 square-mile demilitarized zone (the *despeje*, covering 4 percent of the national territory), an area the size of Switzerland, but with a population of only 96,000 (one-fourth of 1 percent of the national population). A smaller insurgent group, the ELN (*Ejército de Liberación Nacional)* with 5,000 members, may also be given a variant of a demilitarized zone in 2001.

What motivated this unusual arrangement? Because of failed efforts at peace making, especially the execution of thousands of members of the M-19 guerrillas who put down their guns in the early 1990s expecting to be "reintegrated" into society, it was decided that a peace process would work only if the FARC could be assured security in a *despeje*, an area where the government would pull out its police and military forces and allow the FARC local authority.[12] The gesture would show goodwill and establish the basis for meaningful negotiations that would lead to demobilization, eventual reinsertion of members into society, and a durable peace. But the process has achieved little but frustration and criticism, with the result that Pastrana has been able to show hardly anything for his efforts. In the meantime, the FARC has used unfettered control of the *despeje* to recruit, reequip, train, and stage for operations against government forces, as well as promote cultivation of coca. Adopting the classical insurgent strategy of "fight and talk," the FARC continued aggressive military operations against the military and police. Such conduct reinforced the accusation from many quarters at home and abroad that the Colombian government had irresponsibly surrendered sovereignty over Colombian territory to criminals, yielding an important instrument in the struggle for legitimacy.[13]

By the end of 2000, Pastrana had little to show for his gamble in the peace process, and his own standing in national polls plummeted. To preserve the faltering peace process, Pastrana announced in early December that the *despeje* would be maintained until the end of January 2001, and that a humanitarian agreement would free more than 500 Colombian police and army troops held captive in the zone. Ending the *despeje* would amount to ending the peace process, and the government found itself in the untenable position of not being able to retake the zone militarily, so well entrenched is the FARC. [14] Yet there appeared no alternative but to maintain the peace process for both domestic and international reasons. The question was how. Pastrana and Marulanda agreed to another extension via the Los Pozos Accord of February 2001.

Bilaterally, Presidents Bill Clinton and Pastrana hit it off well. Pastrana visited Washington four times, and Clinton journeyed to Cartagena in August 2000 in order to launch Plan Colombia and reassure Colombians of bipartisan support. The presidential retinue included Democratic Senator Joseph Biden and Speaker of the House of Representatives Dennis Hastert. Biden reportedly advised Pastrana: “Mr. President, here are the most powerful men and women in the United States. We believe in you . . . but if there are no results all this good climate could evaporate.”

For some time senior officials in Washington had been thinking that Colombia needed a major boost of U.S. support and a more comprehensive strategy that could be sustained beyond an administration. In November 1999, the U.S. Congress voted a $165 million supplemental aid package for Colombia, which, added to the $124 million appropriated earlier, made Colombia the third-largest recipient (though far behind Israel and Egypt) of U.S. aid in the world. Undersecretary of State Thomas Pickering, an experienced hand in Latin American affairs, argued for a long-term national plan rather than fitful short-term steps that each year had to be repeated in the U.S. political process. It was also imperative that the Colombian government become more proficient in linking a long-term plan with operations in the field and that it mobilize resources and personnel across the ministries, thereby engaging the creative talents of all Colombians in the rebuilding of the nation.

Thus Plan Colombia was born, which, contrary to speculation in the media, was authored by a Colombian—Jaime Ruiz, Chief of Staff for Pastrana, who holds a doctorate from Louvain and an engineering degree from the University of Kansas, has an American wife, and speaks flawless English, wrote the plan in a week in English.[15]

From Strategic Theory to Implementation.

The strategic theory of Plan Colombia is very simple.[16] It links economic development and security to the peace process. The central premise is that drug money feeds the coffers of the guerrillas, whose attacks give rise to the self-defense organizations otherwise known as the paramilitaries. If the money going to the narcos is taken away, the guerrillas cannot mount the attacks, they become less threatening, and the paramilitaries have less reason for being. The prospects for bringing the guerrillas and the paramilitaries to the table for serious peace negotiations are enhanced because they have less justification and less ability to wage war against the state and against each other. Plan Colombia endeavors to strengthen the state, reenergize an economy with deep unemployment, generate the conditions necessary for the pursuit of peace, control the expansion of illegal crops and drug trafficking, and restore civil society. In other words, Plan Colombia is nothing less than a grand strategy for the remaking of the nation into a secure democratic society freed of violence and corruption. It is not a military strategy.

The concept of "shared responsibility" (number 10 of Plan Colombia) for the narcotics problem links with international support. It is common wisdom that little of magnitude happens in this hemisphere without leadership from Washington. Accordingly, U.S. economic and military support is critical in encouraging Colombians to sacrifice for their survival and in prodding the international community to assist. The 5-year Plan Colombia will cost $7.5 billion, with $4 billion to be provided by Colombia, and $3.5 billion by the international community (read here Europe), which includes the $1.3 billion committed by the United States. This division reflects the "shared responsibility" between Colombia and the international community for the problem of drug consumption and production, of demand and supply. Nonetheless, by the end of 2000, European nations, whose understanding of Colombia's complex problems is heavily influenced by human rights-oriented nongovernment organizations, had offered a mere $750 million.[17] Europeans are also reluctant because of the misperception of a heavy military component in the American assistance. In fact, of the U.S. contribution, 61 percent is military.

The main elements of the U.S. aid package for Plan Colombia are:

- Support for human rights and judicial reform — $122 million.

- Expansion of counternarcotics operations in Southern Colombia—$390.5 million (for helicopters, humanitarian assistance, and development assistance).

- Alternative economic development—$81 million for Colombia, $85 million for Bolivia, and $8 million for Ecuador.

- Increased interdiction efforts — $129.4 million.
- Assistance for the Colombian police—$115.6 million.

(These dollars were an emergency supplement to the $330 million earlier provided and $256 million committed for 2001. See Appendix I for more details.)

To give impetus to Plan Colombia, officials from Bogotá and the United States hammered out the *Plan Colombia: Interagency Action Plan*, which is really Annex 1 of Plan Colombia. It is a Colombian project intended to jump-start the first 2 years of the Plan, specifically targeting the high-threat area of Putumayo and Southern Colombia for immediate negative effect on coca production. Its activities will include social actions to promote dignified employment and sustainable development for peasants displaced by the imminent elimination of coca production, the strengthening of the judicial system, the protection of human rights, interdiction of coca shipments in order to isolate production and make legitimate agriculture competitive, and eradication—both voluntary (manual) and aerial. It is hoped that these measures will reduce coca production by 50 percent in 2 years. A comprehensive publicity campaign will promote commitment by the population, generating momentum and mutual confidence between the people and the state agencies. All of the ministries of the national government are involved, as are numerous multilateral agencies such as the United Nations, banks, nongovernmental organizations, as well as various entities of the U.S. Government.[18]

The *Interagency Action Plan* is carefully thought out and comprehensive, and demonstrates the impact of U.S. strategic planning principles (it was a collaborative effort between Colombian officials and U.S. civilian and military planners in summer 2000). It remains to be seen whether the government can muster the political will, the resources, and the organizational skills to implement it. Moreover, the entire country needs the equivalent of the *Interagency Action Plan*, not simply Putumayo and the South.

Linking Strategy to Operations.

Plan Colombia has not been an easy sell. First, there is confusion between the U.S. contribution of $1.3 billion and the $7.5 billion overall plan. Some critics, misreading both Colombia and Vietnam, use what they mistakenly perceive as a similar U.S. experience in South East Asia as a warning. The experience in tiny El Salvador in the 1980s is far more appropriate and applicable to Colombia, though selectively so.

The central component of the U.S. aid package, counternarcotics support, has generated much heat in U.S. intellectual and political circles. A principal point of contention is whether a policy based on counternarcotics will be enough to help Colombia turn the tide against its multiple threats. Shouldn't the United States do more in the form of counterinsurgency? The answer is a resounding no, based on the realities of domestic politics combined with the valuable lessons learned in El Salvador. First, the U.S. Congress will not easily support a counterinsurgency program fraught with controversy. It will more likely support a counternarcotics program. Thus the aid package is the best possible outcome, given the political aversion in the United States to supporting ambiguous wars. Crossing the line into counterinsurgency is simply not an option. Second, unlike El Salvador, Colombia has the resources, if not the political will, to mount and fund its own counterinsurgency. Third, the Colombian government and the armed forces and police, even with all of their inefficiencies, have a greater degree of legitimacy than did the institutions of El Salvador. Finally, counterinsurgency support would be unpopular in Latin America and Europe, and would therefore diminish Colombia's chances of obtaining international support.

The qualified success in El Salvador (which coincided with the twilight of the Cold War, signalling the end of the external Soviet bloc support to the insurgents) was partly due to the prudent decision that the United States would provide only limited indirect support, including the famous 55 advisors, equipment, and training. Salvadorans alone had to make the sacrifices for their own survival, thus putting out strong and more legitimate roots for democracy. U.S. support to Colombia scrupulously avoids counterinsurgency. U.S. trainers from the 7th Special Forces Group will not be with deployed Colombian units. They are on the ground imparting skills to Colombian Army and Navy units. This training will improve the Colombian military's ability to help the Colombian National Police conduct operations against the coca infrastructure.[19] In a typical operation, a Colombian army counternarcotics battalion, vetted specifically for rectitude in human rights and outfitted for light infantry operations, will secure an area from the guerrillas (on the ground as well as air) around a coca facility in order to permit the police to enter safely to arrest, investigate, take evidence, and then destroy the coca and the production facility.

Helicopters provided by the United States (Black Hawks and Hueys) will give much-needed mobility to the three counternarcotics battalions being formed and trained (two battalions were deployed by December 2000). These helicopters are not to be used for counterinsurgency. Because of the long lead time between manufacture, technical modification, the normal pilot training required, and integration with the counternarcotics battalions, the helicopters will not have a significant impact until after mid 2001.[20]

However, neither Colombia nor the United States should be seduced by the promise of technology. While additional helicopters will certainly provide mobility for troops and logistical support, the human element still counts as most important in combat. This verity was demonstrated once again in the FARC shootdown of a

UH-60 Black Hawk helicopter at the battle of Dabeyba in October 2000. The military in this instance failed to conduct adequate reconnaissance.[21]

The 18 Black Hawks and 30 Huey IIs approved for use in Colombia by the U.S. Congress are to be used only for counternarcotics operations, such as force protection, eradication, and lab destruction. They may also be used for humanitarian purposes to prevent the loss of life. Moreover, former Secretary of Defense William Cohen prohibited all Department of Defense "personnel from engaging in actual field operations or deploying to areas where hostile confrontation is imminent."[22]

Whether the distinction between counternarcotics and counterinsurgency operations can be maintained in the fog of the battlefield is another issue. U.S. officials are optimistic that the operational distinction can be made. Also, will counternarcotics operations have lasting results? For example, once a lab or coca field is destroyed, the expectation is that the government will follow-up and provide support (in Spanish, *seguimiento*) to the farmers so that they have a dignified occupational alternative and are integrated into the legitimate economy. That is the objective of the *Inter-Agency Action Plan*. Initial indications were promising. In early December 2000, some 550 families signed up to stop growing coca and instead grow corn, bananas, plantain, palm, yucca, rice, fish, and poultry.[23] Jaime Ruiz, top aide to President Pastrana, commented on the delicate task of convincing peasants:

> If the United States would simply like to finish all the coca in the most cost-effective way—spraying—they would destroy Colombia . . . we are going to tell these people we're going to give them something, not just take something away from them. They have to feel they don't want to grow coca.[24]

Plan Colombia contemplates $88 million for weaning peasants away from growing coca and poppies.

The State Department's Agency for International Development estimates that there are 18,000 small family farms that cultivate about 90,000 acres of coca. How many peasants will be persuaded is uncertain, but if they don't agree, their fields will be sprayed with glyphosate (known in the United States as the weed-killer *Roundup*). Moreover, the bulk of the coca-growing acreage is in the industrial plantations. The owners of these plantations are not traditional farmers, but hardened entrepreneurs directly tied to the international cocaine networks. A tougher approach, forced eradication, will be needed here. Of course, none of this will be permanent unless the government can provide security and economic alternatives and maintain the legal regime in place so that growers do not slip back into bad habits. There are a many "ifs" here, especially the government's ability to sustain programs for the long term.

Alternative development worked to a significant degree in Bolivia (55 percent reduction in 4 years, with even more expected for 2000) and Peru (67 percent). It worked because of a combination of interdiction, eradication, and alternative development that received long-term support from the government. Interdiction and eradication were so effective that the coca economy became unpredictable and, therefore, unattractive to investors. Alternative development worked also because the United States funded the bulk of it. The European reluctance to fully fund their expected contribution to Plan Colombia will set back the alternative development strategy.

Peasants are shrewd capitalists. Amish farmers, for whom smoking is forbidden by their religion, always grow tobacco, a legal crop subsidized by the federal government, in the breadbasket of Lancaster County, Pennsylvania, as a hedge against the weather or a bad market for corn and other crops. Similarly, in Bolivia, peasants take out insurance by planting coca elsewhere.[25] Thus to wean away the peasants permanently, the government needs to maintain both positive and negative incentives for a long time. Columnist George Will is not persuaded that ". . . peace through herbicides . . . to neutralize the left-wing forces by impoverishing them" will work.[26]

Another criticism is that the U.S. support is too generous to the military. Senator Paul Wellstone, after a visit to Colombia (where he and the U.S. Ambassador just missed being bombed), said that giving nearly 75 percent of the aid to the security forces is not a wise choice because "the Colombian military is a deeply troubled institution, even though it has recently taken steps to improve its human rights record."[27]

Even though his percentage is off (the correct figure is 61 percent), Wellstone's critique has company,[28] much like the concerns expressed by the European Parliament and others opposed to the U.S. military assistance. However, this view discounts an important strategic truth. Little will be achieved without security. As the English political theorist John Dunn states, "There cannot be political control without the capacity to coerce."[29] Experience shows that the United States and other donors would be simply throwing money away if the assistance is not secured.

The state's capacity for legitimate coercion will require significant expansion of the armed forces and police. The three counternarcotics battalions themselves will not be enough for that mission. While it won't be total leverage, U.S. policy has enough performance conditions and clout to exact significant human rights compliance by Colombian security forces. This brings forth another key point: U.S. engagement with the government and security forces is fundamental for the humanization of the conflict and for the ultimate success of the government. No other nation has the clout. Madeleine Albright's notion that the United States is the "indispensable" nation, the agent of good, is on the mark for Colombia. Nonetheless, though we can impose accountability, we should not take on burdens that belong to Colombians.

Another strategic reality is that no other nation is willing and able to provide Colombia with the full helicopter package: equipment, training, and maintenance. An unstated principle of international affairs is that the United States makes a political statement of magnitude when it decides through congressional approval to provide military assistance to a beleaguered friend.

Another school of thought criticizes Plan Colombia on the matter of scale. Though they believe that its elements are the right ones, these advocates would support far more international resources for Plan Colombia because as currently configured the plan will only buy time. They would urge the Bush administration to decide that Colombia is the place to draw the line on international crime, adopting the diplomatic equivalent of General Colin Powell's doctrine of "overwhelming force." This would require not only more resources, but even a paradigm shift on the proper use of military forces. None is likely to occur.

Finally, there is the entire decriminalization of drugs school of thought. It is totally opposed to the "war on drugs" at the source. This passionate grouping overlooks the fact that 85 percent of the counternarcotics budget of the United States focuses on demand reduction at home. But even more pertinently, this alternative provides no assurance that narcotics consumption would be reduced. Decriminalization may, in fact, increase it. By a curious coincidence, these activists share ground with the FARC, which stated in March 2000:

> Drug consumption is a lackey of imperialism. . . . We are going to publicly defy North American imperialism so it becomes committed to the legalization of the consumption of drugs, and in this way fight seriously for the elimination of drug trafficking.[30]

Whether this is typical FARC duplicity is a legitimate question. The agreement struck at Los Pozos in February 2001 between Pastrana and 74-year-old Marulanda stated that the FARC would not oppose manual eradication of illicit crops. This seems to have partially met Pastrana's goal of having the FARC denarcotize itself, but it left open the matter of forced eradication of the industrial plantations, a significant source of FARC income.

The bottom line is that Plan Colombia is a well-thought-out set of mutually reinforcing initiatives. It is comprehensive and balanced. So is the U.S. support package. Retired General Charles Wilhelm, who oversaw the genesis of the Colombia commitment as Commander in Chief of the United States Southern Command in Miami between 1997 and 2000, calls Plan Colombia a "social plan with a military support element" and not the other way around. The problem lies not in the design but in the execution, less in Washington and much more in Colombia. The Bush administration will continue the policy of confining support to counternarcotics, refusing to support counterinsurgency. Sustaining the policy for the long haul will be the challenge, for which Colombia must demonstrate enough success to warrant continued U.S. support.

The Colombian government in a sense faces policy overload. It must simultaneously fight three interrelated wars at home against traffickers, insurgents, and paramilitaries. To do so it must generate resources at home and abroad, fully engage the talents of its people, rebuild a totally dysfunctional judicial system, conduct deep reforms of its institutions,[31] sustain the peace process, expand and restructure its armed forces, obtain international support, and rebuild the nation. It must do all of this while subjecting itself to performance conditions from Washington for continued assistance. But that is the inescapable nature of an assistance relationship of mutual dependence. These are extraordinary burdens for a government and society with deep defects. Accordingly, it is critical to answer the question of whether a weak state can function strategically in the Clausewitzian sense. Can Colombia make the link between national level strategy and the implementation of successful operations and tactics?

The crucial question for Colombia is not whether the *Interagency Social Action Plan* is a brilliantly conceived construct—it is—but whether as a nation Colombia can make a commitment to win. Bogotá must mobilize resources for the long term. The violence is not likely to go away in one administration or two. Accordingly, Pastrana and successor leaders across the ministries and decisional elites need to sustain an integrated effort that must begin with the professionalization and expansion of the military as well as the police.[32] Colombia's armed forces must become more proficient in a number of areas: use of intelligence in operations, quick-reaction capability, mobility, logistics, close quarter and night combat, joint operations, medical evacuation, and relations with the civilian population.[33]

The military must also be democratized so that the risk of combat is shared more equally. Until recently the army's *bachilleres* (soldiers with a high school diploma) corps was exempt by law from exposure to combat risk. The corps has been disbanded, but the exemption from combat for those with a secondary education remains law. Thus, before the planned expansion of 55,000 soldiers announced in 2000, nearly 35,000 soldiers were administrative drones in a force of about 135,000 that needed to provide static defense of the infrastructure and respond to simultaneous attacks across an enormous territory. For example, one brigade has to cover the eastern part of Colombia, an area the size of France. The U.S. Army would need a minimum of five divisions for such an area.

Soldiers from the lower class do the fighting and dying. A senior State Department official with intimate on-the-ground knowledge of Colombia asserts that if universal conscription were adopted, the internal wars would be over in 5 years because the middle and upper classes would have a stake in the outcome. Sharing burdens and bounty makes the glue that holds a nation together.[34] The upper and middle classes would demand more money for the military budget, better leadership, better treatment and training, the best equipment for soldiers, and effective strategy and operations. Unfortunately, there is little political support for such a proposal in Colombia. It may be symptomatic of a society in denial of the danger it faces.

Because much of the army is tied down to static defense duty, more units will be needed to pressure the FARC, the ELN, and the paramilitaries. It is unlikely that the insurgents can be defeated militarily, but the balance on the battlefield matters mightily at the peace negotiations. The insurgents have little incentive to negotiate seriously, and the paramilitaries have little rationale to lay down their arms. Once the military establishes a decidedly favorable balance in the field, the other combatants will come to their senses and negotiate rather than await further destruction. Building the peace will not be easy.

In 2000 the army performed very well, according to its commander, General Jorge Enrique Mora. It conducted 3,215 offensive actions, 67 percent more than in 1999, capturing a significant number of guerrillas, paramilitary members, and narco-traffickers.[35] Better leadership was one of the keys for improvements on the battlefield. This was a marked improvement from the 1997-98 period, when the army was losing the war.

Conclusion.

A military effort alone will not bring Colombia back from the brink of total failure as a democracy, but failure is certain without it. History shows that all successful counterinsurgencies in the modern world have had a strong social, economic, and political component to complement the military. The military cannot save Colombia's democratic institutions by itself. There is no alternative to Plan Colombia at this time, and time is of the essence. The Plan provides an excellent foundational strategy that must be further developed, applied to the entire country, and sustained for many years to come. Striking at the source of much of the violence—the narcotics business—is critical for overall success. Given the aversion to counterinsurgency support in the United States, the best this nation can do for

Colombia is reduce its appetite for cocaine and heroin and provide Colombia the "means" and the "know how" to fight its own struggle. The U.S. aversion to counterinsurgency support may actually be in Colombia's best national interest because Colombians will have to make their own sacrifices.

ENDNOTES

1. Ministerio de Defensa Nacional, *El Narcotráfico, una Amenaza para la Seguridad Nacional,* Bogotá, November 2000, p. 1.

2. Inter-American Dialogue, "A Time for Decisions: U.S. Policy in the Western Hemisphere," Washington, DC, 2000, p. 19.

3. For more information on Colombia's complex problems and the U.S. policy dilemmas, see Gabriel Marcella and Donald Schulz, "Colombia's Three Wars: U.S. Strategy at the Crossroads," Carlisle Barracks, PA: Strategic Studies Institute, March 5, 1999; David Passage, "The United States and Colombia: Untying the Gordian Knot," Carlisle Barracks, PA: Strategic Studies Institute, March 2000. See also the report of the Inter-American Dialogue and the Council on Foreign Relations: "Toward Greater Peace and Security in Colombia: Forging a Constructive U.S. Policy," New York: Council on Foreign Relations, 2000. See also *Foreign Affairs en Español*, Vol. 1, No. 1, Spring 2001. Note the articles by Ana Maria Salazar, Luis Alberto Moreno, and Michael Shifter.

4. The spillover effect is not a classical military threat to neighboring countries. It is more a problem of international crime, contraband, corruption, and associated violence. See, for example, Patrice M. Jones, "Colombia's Drug War Spills Into Ecuador," *Chicago Tribune*, February 13, 2001 (*http://ebird.dtic.mil/Feb2001/e20010214colombias.htm*).

5. The balloon effect is more than cultivation. It includes the displacement of trafficking, violence, and consumption into other areas and countries.

6. Hernando Gómez Buendía, "No futuro," *Semana.com*, December 18, 2000 (*http://semana.terra.com.co/972/ZZZT1C5DSGC.asp*). See also the thoughtful commentary by *El Tiempo*'s Rafael Nieto Loaiza, "Las Hipocresias Nacionales," published in *El Tiempo* and personally e-mailed to this author, December 21, 2000.

7. On the threat posed by the paramilitaries, see Ministry of National Defense, *Illegal Self-Defense Groups in Colombia*, Bogotá: December 2000. For a comprehensive treatment of the violence and strategic recommendations from a distinguished military intellectual, see Alvaro Valencia Tovar, *Inseguridad y Violencia en Colombia*, Bogotá: Universidad Sergio Arboleda, 1997.

8. "What this could mean," said Carel De Rooy, "is the proportion of children could be twice what we thought, or they're throwing kids to the front as cannon fodder." Juan Forero, "A Child's Vision of War: Boy Guerrillas In Colombia," *New York Times*, December 20, 2000 (*http://ebird.dtic.mil/Dec2000/e20001220childs.htm*).

9. Juan Forero, "Puerto Asis Journal: To Make a Point, the Rebels Are Strangling a Town," *New York Times*, November 3, 2000 (*nytimes,com/2000/11/03/world/03/COLO.html*); Juan Forero, "Key Roads Taken From Rebels, Colombia Says," November 14, 2000 (*nytimes.com/2000/11/14/world/14COLO.html*).

10. Linda Robinson, Latin American Bureau Chief of *US News and World Report*, maintains that coca accounts for about 50 percent of the FARC income. See Robinson's interview with Warren Olney, National Public Radio International, KCRW, Los Angeles, January 26, 2001.

11. The dysfunctional judicial system and recommended correctives are discussed in Steven Levitt and Mauricio Rubio, "Understanding Crime in Colombia and What Can Be Done About It," Working Paper No. 20, FEDESARROLLO, Bogotá, August 2000.

12. Given the government's inability to control vast areas of Colombia's national territory, there have been de facto *despejes*, areas of practical political autonomy for irregular forces, since independence in the 1820s.

13. See the strong criticism in the *Washington Post* editorial "Crossroads in Colombia," January 3, 2001, p. A16. The distinguished national political leader Noemi Sanín urged a reevaluation and redesign of the peace process. See her letter to FARC leader Manuel Marulanda in "Hay que rediseñar el proceso de paz," *El Tiempo*, January 7, 2001, *http://eltiempo.terra.com.co/07-01-2001/paza*.

14. Undersecretary of State Thomas Pickering remarked, "It is not possible to defend the existence of the *despeje* when there are no negotiations." Scott Wilson, "To Preserve Peace Talks, Colombia Maintains DMZ," *Washington Post*, December 7, 2000 (*washingtonpost.com/ac2/wp-dyn/A38377-2000Dec7*).

15. Source of this information is former Ambassador to Colombia, Curtis Kamman. Interview, U.S. Army War College, Carlisle, PA, December 8, 2000. Writing it in English may have been a tactical blunder that helped fuel rumors that Washington wrote Plan Colombia.

16. The full title of the plan is *Plan Colombia: Plan for Peace, Prosperity, and the Strengthening of the State*. It is available in English and Spanish from the Colombian Presidency: *http://www.presidencia.gov.co/webpresi/plancolo/plancin2.htm*.

17. Howard LaFranchi, "Briefing: Putumayo, The Newest Front In the Latin Drug War," *Christian Science Monitor*, December 12, 2000; (*http://ebird.dtic.mil/Dec2000/e20001212newest.htm*). The European Parliament qualifies its support of Plan Colombia: "stepping up military involvement in the fight against drugs risks sparking off an escalation of the conflict in the region, and . . . military solutions cannot bring about lasting peace." Its 22-point statement, "European Parliament Resolution on Plan Colombia and Support for the Peace Process in Colombia," available from *ceudes@andinet.com*. The European Parliament in February voted 474 to 1 against supporting Plan Colombia because it was a bilateral agreement between Bogota and Washington. The Parliament's action was mainly a psychological gesture, lacking any policy authority.

18. More details can be found in Office of the President, *Plan Colombia: Interagency Action Plan*, Phase I, Bogotá, 2000.

19. The total number of U.S. military trainers fluctuates between 200 and 300, with a limit of 500. Civilian contract trainers number about 300. Obviously some of the principles of instruction and skills imparted via U.S. trainers apply to both counternarcotics and counterinsurgency. The expectation is that such training will have a professionalizing impact throughout the army.

20. On this, see United States General Accounting Office, "Drug Control: U.S. Assistance to Colombia Will Take Years to Produce Results," Report to the Chairman and Ranking Member, Subcommittee on Criminal Justice, Drug Policy, and Human Resources, Committee on Government Reform, House of Representatives, Washington, DC, October 2000. See also the testimony of Jess T. Ford before the same subcommittee, "Drug Control: Challenges in Implementing Plan Colombia," October 12, 2000.

21. See Karen DeYoung, "Colombia Plan Faces 'Crunch Time,'" *Washington Post*, December 22, 2000; *http://Washingtonpost.com/wp-dyn/articles/A38415-2000Dec21.html*.

22. Information provided by LTC George Rhynedance, Public Affairs, Office of the Assistant Secretary of Defense, August 31, 2000.

23. The difficulties of crop eradication based on spraying, crop substitution, and winning the hearts and minds of peasants who have felt that they have been abandoned by the government should not be minimized. See Juan Forero, "Luring Colombian Farmers from Coca Cash Crop," *New York Times*, November 20, 2000; *nytimes.com/2000/11/20/ world/20COCA*; Juan Forero, "No Crops Spared in Colombia's Coca War," *New York Times*, January 31, 2001, pp. A1, A8; David Adams, "Plan Colombia Gets Off to Rocky Start," *St. Petersburg Times*, February 11, 2001; *sptimes.com/News/021101/ Worldandnation/Plan Colombia gets of.shtml*; David Adams and Jared Kotler, "In War On Coca, Colombia Enlists Farmers," *Philadelphia Inquirer*, December 5, 2000; *http://ebird.dtic.mil/Dec20001205inwar.htm.* The aggressive Bolivian coca eradication and crop substitution program in the Chapare has caused widespread resentment among peasant farmers, though the Hugo Banzer government promises to leave Bolivia without drugs by 2002. See Clifford Krauss, "Bolivia Wiping Out Coca, at a Price," *New York Times*, October 23, 2000; *nytimes.com/2000/10 /23/world/ 23BOLI.html.*

24. Karen DeYoung, "A Long Way from Coca to Coffee," *Washington Post*, October 11, 2000, p. A18.

25. The success in Bolivia is far from complete. While most of the cultivation in the Chapare had been eliminated (all but a few hundred hectares) by the end of 2000, the "legal" growth in the Yungas has expanded to some 12,000 hectares. See *The Economist*, January 6, 2001, pp. 31-32.

26. George F. Will, "Colombia Illusions," *Washington Post*, September 10, 2000, p. B7.

27. Paul Wellstone, "Bush Should Start Over in Colombia," *New York Times*, December 26, 2000 (*nytimes.com/2000/12/26/opinion*). For a scholarly analysis of the interplay between the military and the new threats, see Cynthia A. Watson, "Civil-Military Relations in Colombia: A Workable Relationship or a Case for Fundamental Reform?" *Third World Quarterly*, Vol. 21, No. 3, 2000, pp. 529-548. The army's improved human rights conduct can be seen in the Department of State's annual *Country Reports on Human Rights Practices*, for example, 1997, 1998, and 1999. The military's ties to the paramilitaries, tacit and active, still are strongly criticized, even by U.S. officials.

28. See, for example, Adam Isacson, "U.S. Military Aid to Colombia: The Human Rights Implications," Washington: Center for International Policy, 2000.

29. John Dunn, *The Cunning of Unreason: Making Sense of Politics*, London: Basic Books, 2000, p. 120.

30. *Document of FARC Plenum*, March 21-25, 2000, location unknown. Decriminalization has other and more nuanced exponents. For example, Clinton's drug czar, retired General Barry McCaffrey, and Governor Gary E. Johnson of New Mexico advocate modifying laws to reduce mandatory incarceration of some drug consumers, better education, care and rehabilitation, thus refusing to "tolerate the needless casualties of drug prohibition." See Gary E. Johnson, "Another Prohibition: Another Failure," *New York Times, http://www.nytimes.com/2000/12/30/opinion/30John.html.*

31. Among the reforms it must undertake is the overhauling of the entire apparatus of government and the constitution, and decentralize administration. See the recommendations in Alberto Alesina, Alberto Carrasquilla, and Juan José Echavarría, "Decentralization in Colombia," FEDESARROLLO, Working Paper No. 15, Bogotá, August 2000; Alberto Alesina, "Institutional Reforms in Colombia," FEDESARROLLO, Working Paper No. 21, Bogotá, November 2000.

32. According to former Defense Minister Rafael Pardo Rueda, the country needs a lot more policemen. As many as 200 municipalities may be without police. See Pardo's "En vez de paramilitares más policía," *El Espectador,* January 18, 2001; accessed via internet.

33. For more specific analysis on the needs of the Colombian military, see Passage, "The United States and Colombia: Untying the Gordian Knot."

34. On this concept, see the profound meditation by Deborah Stone, *Policy Paradox: The Art of Political Decision Making*, New York: Norton, 1997, p. 20.

35. See General Mora's report in "Capturados 1,018 guerrilleros en el año 2000," *El Tiempo*, January 2, 2001, p. A1.

APPENDIX I

SPECIFIC ELEMENTS OF U.S. SUPPORT TO COLOMBIA

A. Alternative Economic Development and Resettlement: alternative crops, applied research on crops with identified markets, credit and land titling, and productive infrastructure (such as packing sheds, storage, and drainage), environmental programs, local governance, assistance to internally displaced people with infrastructure projects (schoolrooms, water systems, roads and bridges, and market shelters).

B. Improving Governing Capacity: protection of human rights workers, strengthening human rights institutions, establishing human rights task forces, child soldier rehabilitation, witness and judicial security in human rights cases, support of the United Nations human rights office and U.S. Government monitoring.

C. Administration of Justice: reform of criminal code, prosecutor training, judge training, judicial centers, public defenders.

D. Law enforcement: asset forfeiture/money laundering task force, anti-corruption program, financial crime investigating units, anti-kidnapping strategy, judicial police training academy, custom police training, maritime enforcement and port security, multilateral law enforcement, prison security, banking supervision assistance, revenue enhancement assistance, customs training assistance, investigation and prosecution of organized financial crime, military human rights and legal reform, the Army Judge Advocate General School.

E. Support for the Peace Process: seminars and analysis of conflict management and comparative peace processes.

APPENDIX II

THE TEN ELEMENTS OF PLAN COLOMBIA

1. *An economic strategy* that generates employment, supports the ability of the State to collect tax revenues and allows the country to have a viable counterbalancing economic force to narco-trafficking. The expansion of international trade, accompanied by enhanced access to foreign markets and free trade agreements to attract foreign and domestic investment are key to the modernization of our economic base and to job creation. Such a strategy is crucial at a time when Colombia is confronting its worst economic crisis in 70 years, with unemployment running 20 percent, which in turn greatly limits the government's ability to confront drug trafficking and the violence it generates.

2. *A fiscal and financial strategy* that includes tough austerity and adjustment in order to boost economic activity and recover the historically excellent prestige of Colombia in international financial markets.

3. *A peace strategy* that aims at a negotiated peace agreement with the guerrillas on the basis of territorial integrity, democracy and human rights, which should further strengthen the rule of law and the fight against drugs.

4. *A national defense strategy* to restructure and modernize the armed forces and the police, so that they will be able to restore the rule of law and provide security in the country, to combat organized crime and armed groups and to protect and promote human rights and international humanitarian law.

5. *A judicial and human rights strategy* to reaffirm the rule of law and assure equal and impartial justice to all,

while pressing ahead with the reforms already initiated in the forces of law and order to ensure that they play their proper role in defending and respecting the rights and dignity of all.

6. A *counternarcotics strategy*, in partnership with other countries involved in some or all of the links of the drug chain: production, distribution, sale, consumption, asset laundering, precursor chemicals, and arms dealing. And, at the national level, to stop the flow of drug money—the fuel of violence—to the insurgent and other armed organizations.

7. *An alternative development strategy* that will promote agricultural schemes and other profitable economic activities for peasant farmers and their families. Alternative development will also consider economically feasible environmental protection activities, designed to conserve the forest areas and end the dangerous expansion of illegal crops across the Amazon basin and Colombia's vast national parks—areas of immense bio-diversity of vital environmental importance to the international community. Within this framework the strategy includes sustainable, integrated, and participatory productive projects combined with the required infrastructure. Particular attention is to regions which combine high levels of conflict with low levels of State presence, social capital, and serious environmental degradation, such as the Middle Magdalena valley, the *Macizo Colombiano,* and the south-west.

8. *A social participation strategy* aimed at collective awareness. The strategy seeks to develop more accountability in local government, community involvement in anticorruption efforts, and continued pressure on the guerrillas and other armed groups to end kidnapping, violence and the internal displacement of individuals and communities. The strategy will also include cooperation with local business and labor groups, in order to promote innovative and productive models in the face of a more globalized economy. In addition, this strategy seeks to strengthen institutions, both formal and informal, to foster

changes in the cultural patterns through which violence develops and reinforces itself. It includes the promotion of mechanisms and educational programs to increase tolerance, the essential values for peaceful coexistence, and participation in public affairs.

9. *A human development strategy* to promote efforts to guarantee, within the next few years, adequate education and health, to provide opportunities to every young Colombian and help vulnerable groups in our society, including not just those affected and displaced by violence but also those in conditions of extreme poverty.

10. *An international oriented strategy* to confirm the principles of shared responsibility, integrated action and balanced treatment of the drug issue. The role and support of the international community is also vital to the success of the peace process provided that it conforms to the terms of international law and is requested by the Colombian government.

U.S. ARMY WAR COLLEGE

Major General Robert R. Ivany
Commandant

*****

Author
Dr. Gabriel Marcella
Department of National and International
Security Studies

*****

STRATEGIC STUDIES INSTITUTE

Director
Professor Douglas C. Lovelace, Jr.

Director of Research
Dr. Earl H. Tilford, Jr.

Director of Publications and Production
Ms. Marianne P. Cowling

Publications Assistant
Ms. Rita A. Rummel

****

Composition
Mrs. Christine A. Williams

Cover Artist
Mr. James E. Kistler

www.ingramcontent.com/pod-product-compliance
Ingram Content Group UK Ltd.
Pitfield, Milton Keynes, MK11 3LW, UK
UKHW041901190726
13854UKWH00003B/1030